THE SUPERSTAR SQUAD
The Mysterious Case of the Missing Smile

BLUME POTTER

INTRODUCTION

Welcome to the enchanting world of The Superstar Squad! This delightful book series is more than just a collection of stories—it's a journey into the heart of friendship, kindness, and the joy of discovering one's unique talents.

In The Superstar Squad, your child or grandchild will meet a diverse group of animal friends, including Luna the Rabbit, Ziggy the Squirrel, Pepper the Parrot, and Oliver the Owl. These charming characters use their unique skills and teamwork to overcome obstacles and spread happiness wherever they go. Each story is written in a witty and engaging prose style, perfect for young readers aged 3 to 8.

Through their adventures, the Superstar Squad teaches valuable life lessons about empathy, the power of kindness, and the importance of embracing individuality. These stories are designed to not only entertain but also to educate and inspire young minds, fostering a love for reading and a deeper understanding of what it means to be a good friend.

In The Mysterious Case of the Missing Smile, the Squad embarks on a heartfelt quest to help Oliver the Owl regain his lost smile. As they navigate through challenges and uncover clues, they demonstrate the true power of friendship and the magic that happens when we support and uplift each other.

This book is a perfect addition to bedtime routines, family reading time, or any moment when you want to share the joy of a beautifully crafted story. It's a gift that keeps on giving, providing your child or grandchild with the tools to grow into a kind, confident, and compassionate individual.

Join Luna, Ziggy, Pepper, and Oliver on their captivating adventures, and let the Superstar Squad bring a smile to your loved ones' faces—one story at a time.

Happy reading!

CHAPTER 1:
THE DISAPPEARING SMILE

The meadow was alive with laughter and fun as the Superstar Squad played their favorite games. Luna the Rabbit hopped around joyfully, Ziggy the Squirrel raced up and down the trees, and Pepper the Parrot flew in loops, showing off her colorful feathers. But today, something was different.

"Hey, where's Oliver?" Luna asked, pausing mid-hop.

The Squad looked around and spotted Oliver the Owl sitting quietly under a big oak tree. Normally, Oliver's face would light up with a big smile whenever he saw his friends. But today, his eyes looked sad, and there was no smile to be found.

Luna bounded over, her nose twitching with concern. "Oliver, are you okay? You seem a little down."

Oliver sighed and shook his head. "I don't know, Luna. I just woke up today, and my smile was gone."

Pepper fluttered down and perched on a low branch. "That's strange! Smiles don't just disappear, do they?"

Ziggy chattered, "We have to find your smile, Oliver! The Superstar Squad can solve anything together!"

The friends gathered around, forming a circle of determination. They knew that when one of them was in trouble, they all pitched in to help. Luna, as the natural leader, started brainstorming.

"Let's think about what might have happened," she said. "Oliver, did anything unusual happen yesterday?"

Oliver tilted his head, thinking hard. "Not really, just the usual day. I read my favorite book, played with you all, and then went home for dinner."

Luna's ears perked up. "What about your dinner? Was it different?"

Oliver shook his head. "Nope, just my favorite berries and nuts."

Pepper squawked, "Maybe you lost your smile somewhere! We need to retrace your steps."

Ziggy clapped his tiny paws. "Great idea, Pepper! Let's go back to all the places Oliver visited yesterday."

The Squad decided to start their search at the meadow where they played the day before. They combed through the grass, looked under rocks, and even checked inside the bushes. But no smile.

Next, they went to the big oak tree where Oliver liked to read. They checked every branch and leaf, but still no smile.

As the sun began to set, the Squad grew tired but not discouraged. "We won't give up, Oliver," Luna said with a determined hop. "Tomorrow, we'll keep looking. We'll figure out this mystery together."

Oliver felt a little better knowing his friends were there for him. He managed a small, grateful grin. "Thanks, everyone. I know we'll find my smile soon."

As they all headed home, the Squad was more determined than ever to solve the mysterious case of the missing smile. They knew that with teamwork and kindness, they could brighten even the darkest day.

CHAPTER 2:
CLUES IN THE DARK

The next morning, the Superstar Squad gathered bright and early in the meadow, ready to continue their search. Oliver the Owl was there too, still looking a bit down but hopeful.

Luna the Rabbit, with her ears perked up, started the meeting. "Okay, everyone, we need to think about anything unusual that might have happened to Oliver. We already checked the places he went yesterday. Maybe we should think about what happened during the night."

Ziggy the Squirrel nodded enthusiastically. "Good idea, Luna! Oliver, did anything weird happen last night?"

Oliver blinked his big eyes. "Now that you mention it, I did have a strange dream."

Pepper the Parrot flapped her wings excitedly. "Tell us about the dream, Oliver! Maybe it's a clue!"

Oliver thought back to the night before. "Well, I dreamed I was flying high in the night sky, chasing after a big, glowing star. It was beautiful, but no matter how fast I flew, I couldn't catch it. Then, suddenly, the star turned into a big, dark cloud, and I woke up feeling... empty."

Luna tapped her chin thoughtfully. "That's definitely unusual. Dreams can sometimes tell us important things. Maybe the star and the cloud mean something."

Ziggy chattered, "Maybe the cloud took your smile! We should try to understand what the dream means."

Pepper squawked, "I know someone who can help! My cousin, Pablo the Parrot, knows a lot about dreams. He lives in the old oak tree on the other side of the forest."

The Squad agreed to visit Pablo. They made their way through the forest, chattering and fluttering with determination. When they reached the old oak tree, Pablo was there, preening his bright feathers.

"Pablo!" Pepper called out. "We need your help with a dream mystery!"

Pablo looked down from his perch with wise eyes. "Tell me about the dream, Oliver."

Oliver repeated his dream about the glowing star and the dark cloud. Pablo listened carefully, nodding his head.

"Hmm," Pablo said thoughtfully. "The star represents something you cherish, something that makes you happy. The dark cloud might symbolize a worry or fear that is covering your happiness."

Luna's eyes widened. "So, if we figure out what's worrying Oliver, we might find his smile?"

Pablo nodded. "Exactly. Oliver, do you remember feeling worried about anything recently?"

Oliver thought hard. "Well, I've been a little worried about the storm that's coming. I heard it might be a big one, and storms always make me nervous."

Luna hopped closer. "That makes sense! Maybe thinking about the storm is what's making you feel down. But remember, Oliver, we're all here to help you. We can face the storm together."

Ziggy clapped his tiny paws. "Yeah! We'll make sure you're safe and happy, no matter what!"

Pepper flapped her wings. "And we can think of fun things to do inside if the storm comes!"

Oliver felt a bit of hope returning. "Thanks, everyone. Just talking about it makes me feel a little better."

The Squad spent the rest of the day making a plan for the storm. They gathered cozy blankets, found fun indoor games, and made sure Oliver knew he wasn't alone.

As the day ended, Oliver felt lighter. His smile hadn't completely returned, but he felt it was closer now. He thanked his friends for their help and support.

"Tomorrow," Luna said with a confident hop, "we'll keep searching for your smile. We're getting closer, Oliver. I can feel it."

With a renewed sense of determination, the Superstar Squad headed home, ready to continue their quest. They knew that with teamwork, they could solve any mystery and bring back Oliver's smile.

CHAPTER 3:
THE STORMY NIGHT

The sky grew dark as the storm approached, casting long shadows over the meadow. The Superstar Squad gathered at Oliver's cozy treehouse, determined to stay close and help him face his fear of the storm.

Inside the treehouse, the Squad made everything as cozy as possible. Luna the Rabbit arranged soft blankets and pillows in a corner, while Ziggy the Squirrel set up a small lantern that cast a warm, comforting glow. Pepper the Parrot perched on a low branch, her colorful feathers adding cheer to the room.

Oliver the Owl watched his friends with gratitude. "Thanks for staying with me, everyone. Storms always make me nervous, but it's better with you all here."

Luna hopped over and gave Oliver a reassuring pat. "We're a team, Oliver. We face everything together."

As the first raindrops tapped against the window, the Squad settled in. They decided to share stories to pass the time and keep Oliver's mind off the storm. Luna started with a funny tale about a rabbit who tried to outsmart a sneaky fox, making everyone laugh.

Next, Ziggy shared a story about his adventures collecting the best acorns in the forest. He acted out the parts, scampering around the treehouse and making everyone giggle.

Pepper flapped her wings and told a story about a parrot who wanted to learn to sing like a nightingale. Her mimicry of the bird's song was so perfect that it filled the treehouse with beautiful melodies.

Oliver couldn't help but smile as he listened to his friends. Despite the storm raging outside, he felt safe and happy inside the treehouse.

Just then, a loud clap of thunder shook the treehouse, and the wind howled through the trees. Oliver shivered, but Luna was quick to hop over and sit beside him.

"Remember, Oliver, we're all here. The storm can't hurt us."

Ziggy nodded, his eyes bright with determination. "And think of all the fun we're having! We're making new memories together."

Pepper added, "We can make a game out of it! Every time we hear thunder, we'll cheer and clap our hands."

As the storm continued, the Squad kept their spirits high with more stories and games. They even sang songs, their voices blending harmoniously and creating a joyful noise that drowned out the storm.

In the midst of all the fun, Oliver felt a warmth spreading through his heart. He realized that his friends' support and love were more powerful than any storm. They made him feel brave and safe.

During a brief moment of calm, when the rain had lessened and the thunder was distant, Oliver looked around at his friends. "You know, I was so worried about the storm that I forgot how wonderful it feels to be with all of you. Your stories, your laughter... they've brought back a bit of my smile."

Luna's eyes twinkled. "That's the magic of friendship, Oliver. We're always here to help each other, no matter what."

Ziggy scampered over and gave Oliver a tiny acorn. "This is a lucky acorn. It's a reminder that even in the toughest times, we have each other."

Pepper fluttered down and nuzzled Oliver gently. "And remember, Oliver, smiles come from the heart. Yours will be back fully in no time."

As the night wore on, the storm gradually subsided. The Squad fell asleep in the cozy treehouse, feeling the warmth of their friendship all around them.

Oliver drifted off to sleep with a peaceful heart, his smile slowly returning. He knew that with friends like Luna,

Ziggy, and Pepper, he could face any challenge and find his way back to happiness.

CHAPTER 4:
THE SECRET MESSAGE

The next morning, the sky was clear and bright, a sharp contrast to the stormy night before. The Superstar Squad woke up in Oliver's cozy treehouse, feeling refreshed and hopeful. They were determined to continue their quest to bring back Oliver's smile.

As they stepped outside, Luna noticed something unusual in the dirt near the treehouse. "Hey, look over here!" she called to her friends.

The Squad gathered around and saw strange markings in the dirt. It looked like someone had written a message. Ziggy, with his sharp eyes, read it aloud. "Follow the trail to the heart of the forest, where secrets and smiles are stored."

Pepper flapped her wings excitedly. "It's a clue! Maybe Oliver's smile left this message to help us find it."

Oliver's eyes widened. "Do you really think so? That would be amazing!"

Luna nodded. "It's worth a try. Let's follow the trail and see where it leads."

The Squad set off, following the faint trail marked by small stones and broken twigs. The path led them deeper into the forest, where the trees grew taller and the air was filled with the songs of birds.

As they walked, they chatted about the adventures they'd had and the fun they'd shared. Oliver felt his spirits lifting with each step, surrounded by his caring friends.

After a while, the trail led them to a clearing in the heart of the forest. In the center of the clearing was a large, ancient tree with a hollow trunk. The tree seemed to glow with a gentle light, making it look magical.

"Wow," Ziggy whispered, his eyes wide with wonder. "This place feels special."

Pepper perched on a low branch and looked around. "Maybe this is where secrets and smiles are stored!"

Luna approached the tree and peered into the hollow trunk. "There's something inside!" she exclaimed, reaching in and pulling out a small, wooden box.

The box was beautifully carved with intricate patterns and seemed to hum with a soft, soothing energy. Oliver's heart pounded with anticipation as Luna handed him the box.

"Open it, Oliver," Luna encouraged with a bright smile.

Oliver took a deep breath and carefully opened the box. Inside, nestled on a bed of soft moss, was a small, glowing orb. The light from the orb was warm and inviting, and as Oliver held it, he felt a surge of happiness.

"It's my smile!" Oliver exclaimed, his eyes lighting up with joy. "I can feel it!"

The Squad cheered and gathered around Oliver, their faces beaming with happiness. "We did it!" Ziggy said, clapping his tiny paws.

Pepper squawked happily. "Teamwork and friendship saved the day!"

Oliver placed the glowing orb close to his heart, and as he did, he felt his smile returning fully. It wasn't just a physical smile; it was a deep, genuine happiness that filled him from head to toe.

Luna hopped over and hugged Oliver. "We knew we'd find it, Oliver. Your smile was always there, just waiting for you to find it with a little help from your friends."

Ziggy nodded. "And now, you can keep it safe and bright, knowing we're always here for you."

Oliver felt tears of joy welling up in his eyes. "Thank you, everyone. I couldn't have done it without you. You've shown me how powerful friendship and kindness really are."

The Squad spent the rest of the day in the magical clearing, celebrating their success and enjoying each other's company. They laughed, played games, and shared stories, knowing that their bond had grown even stronger.

As the sun began to set, they headed back to the meadow, their hearts full of joy and their spirits high. Oliver's smile was brighter than ever, and he knew that with friends like Luna, Ziggy, and Pepper, he could face any challenge and find happiness in even the darkest times.

SUPERSTAR SQUAD

CHAPTER 5:
THE POWER OF FRIENDSHIP

As the Superstar Squad made their way back to the meadow, the air was filled with a sense of accomplishment and joy. Oliver's smile was back, shining brightly, and their adventure had brought them even closer together.

When they arrived at the meadow, they gathered in their favorite spot under the big oak tree. The sun was setting, casting a warm golden glow over the meadow, making it the perfect time for reflection.

Luna the Rabbit hopped onto a rock and looked at her friends with a proud smile. "We did it, everyone. We found Oliver's smile! But more importantly, we did it together."

Ziggy the Squirrel nodded, his eyes sparkling. "Yeah, and we learned a lot about each other along the way. Like how we can turn a scary storm into a fun night just by being there for each other."

Pepper the Parrot flapped her wings and perched on a low branch. "And how even a strange dream can lead us to the right path when we work together and support one another."

Oliver the Owl, his heart full of gratitude, spoke up. "I want to thank you all. You showed me that no matter how tough things get, I'm never alone. You helped me find my smile again, and I'll never forget that."

Luna's eyes twinkled. "That's the magic of the Superstar Squad. Our friendship and teamwork can solve any mystery, overcome any fear, and bring back any lost smile."

Ziggy clapped his tiny paws. "We're stronger together, and that's what makes us special."

Pepper added, "And we'll always be here for each other, no matter what."

The Squad decided to celebrate their success with a little party. They gathered some of their favorite snacks—berries, nuts, and seeds—and shared a delicious picnic under the oak tree. They sang songs, played games, and laughed until their sides ached.

As the stars began to twinkle in the night sky, Luna suggested they each say something they appreciated about their adventure.

Luna started. "I appreciated how we all worked together and never gave up, even when things seemed tough."

Ziggy said, "I loved how we turned a scary storm into a night of fun and friendship."

Pepper added, "I'm thankful for Pablo's wisdom and how it helped us understand the clues."

Oliver, his heart full, said, "I'm grateful for each one of you. You've shown me the true power of friendship and how it can bring light to the darkest times."

They all agreed that their adventure had made their bond stronger and that they were ready for any challenge that might come their way in the future.

As they lay under the stars, ready to drift off to sleep, Luna had one last thought. "Remember, everyone, our friendship is our greatest strength. As long as we stick together, we can make the world a brighter place."

The Squad nodded in agreement, feeling a deep sense of contentment. They knew that the Superstar Squad wasn't just a group of friends; it was a family bound by love, kindness, and the power to bring smiles wherever they went.

With hearts full of happiness, they fell asleep under the twinkling stars, dreaming of future adventures and the joy of their unbreakable bond. And in the gentle night breeze, Oliver's smile shone as bright as ever, a testament to the enduring magic of friendship.